I0755940

FINISHING LINE PRESS
www.finishinglinepress.com

LOAD-BEARING WALLS

poems by

Linda B. Myers

Finishing Line Press
Georgetown, Kentucky

LOAD-BEARING WALLS

ISBN 979-8-89990-409-7 First Edition

ACKNOWLEDGMENTS

Poems in this collection have appeared, in earlier versions, in the following:

"Last Gift" and "Fatalities in the North Cascades" in *Cirque Literary Journal*
"Peninsula Currents" in the gallery presentation of Port Angeles Fine Arts Center, 2023
"Transcatheter Aortic Valve Replacement" in *Madrona Anthology* published by Empty Bowl
"Playing Henry Fonda on a Humid Afternoon," "Load-Bearing Walls (former title "Sanctuary for Old Women,") and "Tattoo Jungle" in *Unleash Lit*

Publisher: Leah Huete de Maines
Editor: Christen Kincaid
Cover Art: Shutterstock_2559594009.jpg
Author Photo: Judith R. Duncan
Cover Design: Elizabeth Maines McCleavy

Order online: www.finishinglinepress.com
also available on amazon.com

Author inquiries and mail orders:
Finishing Line Press
PO Box 1626
Georgetown, Kentucky 40324
USA

Contents

To all the load-bearing walls
who support one another

LAST GIFT

Dead people
visit hospice rooms as other lives end.
Mostly ghostly mothers
console their grown-old young.

For my husband
it was dogs
tumbling, leaping, galloping
into his room that final day.
Mutts and purebreds
spaniels and wieners
paid for and rescued
all the good girls and boys
we raised in our days together
the mister and me.

Screaming Yellow Zonker,
Northern Cider, Jack the Ripper,
Lizzie Borden, Maggie J, Wheeler,
Max, and poor little Charlie
yipping, yapping, growling, howling,
each according to their nature.

Their man too sick to throw sticks,
each dog too long gone to fetch,
but they came as a pack
to escort him on his way.
Those wagging tongues and tails
gifted him with joy,
and he to me in his last telling
before the fade.

AN UNKINDNESS OF WORDS

"You used to be fun."
    If you mean I won't go to Branson with your family again
    and I resent you calling my breasts fun bags,
    then yes, I've grown dull. I'll go my own way
    while you cheer TV sports with teams I never heard of.

"You've really let yourself go."
    I've let myself go tend my needs as well as yours.
    You sag too, you know, your knees crackle as you step.
    Your ears now deafened by heartlessness no longer hear
    the sweet, only the nothings.

"You've never understood me."
    Oh, please.

"I don't love you anymore."
    I am crazed as an old enamel vase laced with blue veins,
    but the vessel and I both still hold water. Tell me
    Mr. Guitar Man, how can you pluck all these years
    never mastering an actual song?

"You've seen the last of me."
    Not quite. You forgot snot rags wadded on the counter,
    towels damp with your scent, crusted toothpaste tube.
    You left your detritus like mini-suicide notes
    for me to discover and place in the trash.

ISLAND AUNTIES

I uncovered that hot pink comb today
the one from the off-brand pharmacy
haoles wouldn't find or favor if they did.

Plastic pick one end, sharp teeth the other
foldable to tuck into a tropical hibiscus tote.
We gave it a go, your black Polynesian
Chinese curls thick with defiance
while my limp blonde mop, the only thing
about me that's ever been thin,
surrendered as spines shredded my head.

How you loved to barter for a priceless
black pearl or last season's muumuu.
It mattered not. What mattered
is how I sidekicked in your shadow
led astray by a six-foot-two Pele lookalike.

I was laughter on a second scooter
flashing through Makalapua Mall
two crazy aunties careening
into Macy's underpants department
to replenish your old size tens with slinky sixes
after your weight washed away
in a toxic stream of too many ills, too many pills.

You gave me that comb. And pearls. And glee.
Then you died as hard as you lived.
The island fires are the second time
Hawaii broke my heart.

LOAD-BEARING WALLS

Consider my starting point:
Body beached wreckage, knee bent as driftwood.
Mind blurry about little things like time.
Age wages its own kind of war

but ye gods! I still ignite like a bonfire
searing the Phoenix that doesn't lift its feet fast enough.
I fume at women voting for a man
who grabbed them by the offending word.
At caging brown babies.
At justices who are not.
I shake my arthritic fist until even I
am tired of me.

So here I sit shunted to the side of the road.
The world I knew is gone. A helluva thing.
I struggle up, trudge on, a refugee
dropping mama's scrapbook
heirloom cups
boudoir chair
treasure by treasure
left at the curb on the way to someplace new

and in the oddest place, I find it.
Sanctuary for old women.
Load-bearing walls for each other. We listen,
take strength from those overcoming damage
as we overcome our own.
We pluck out time-worn troubles
like tick heads yanked with tweezers

and light each other's campfires,
tend the flames until we rise
not spreading our wings as wide as the great bird
I thought might be dead: but that thing with feathers
hasn't flown from us yet.

AS CAULDRONS EXPLODE

She carries death in her head.
In caverns and organs buried deep
explosion trembles on the brink.

Liver, lung, kidney, spleen.
Magnitude Intensity Eruption
Lava rivers blistering upward.

Emergency preparedness fails.
Useless to chop or syphon or store.
Bottle nothing but tears.

Into her skull rot rushes and pools.
Brain tumor building up muscle.
MRIs official.

This earth, this girl will tear apart.
Eruption through rock and gristle
as cauldrons explode, tumors unfurl.

Disposable world. Disposable girl.

PLEASURE CRUISE

My eyes circle the white dining room. Over the rim
of my Delftware cup I discover her. She is ageless.
Heirloom elegant. Ships could sail by the light of her glow.
Above the brioche crumbs, she says her name is Doris

changed from Dixie in a snit at those damn Texans.
She is animated as a Chopin étude, dressed in radiance
and white linen but for the enormous red silk rose,
gaudy with rhinestones pinned to her chest.

She shows no sign she doesn't know me. I ask about
her rose. "Red for departure, purple for return. We are
just on our way. Tomorrow we stroll beaches in Aloha
shirts and slippahs, fly Napali coast, swim with whales."

In time, her husband rises, ruffles her cotton boll hair,
kisses her pink chamois cheek, whispers as they depart
"Thank you. She has lost her mind, you know."
Of course she has. This ship sails to Panama.

Only Dixie is on her way to the islands. I am happy to
travel along. She is a plundered buffet, now lost to
old friends. I never met that Dixie. What remains
uplifts me like a fragile luna moth in its final stage.

FATALITIES IN THE NORTH CASCADES

I.

Wildfire chars bark and other wild skins
crisp as chicharrónes.
Trunks stripped naked topple down hillsides.
Music of the forest has flown. I listen for hearts,
sprouts, spoors, fireweed and fiddleheads to mend.
Is this metaphor for my country's uncontrolled burn
or foretelling of my own ignited anger?

II.

I've crossed the fog line.
I can't find up
in this ghost grey ocean of sky.
Distant voices whisper stories
from my eulogy.
As I face the river, fog lifts.
I remove the peel from an orange.

III.

I recall another fallen tree in another forest.
Nurse log for a decade of kids
who rode her like an elephant
loving her broad back and burl-knot head.

IV.

Rules of migration may bring
Western tanagers back one day
yellow melody brighter than a burn.

PHONE GHOST

I carried Barry
in my phone
until it too died.
If a smartphone's
worth its name
his ghost transferred
to the new.
It's the least
an Apple can do.

He was immense
cedar strong
a bellow of laughter
his chosen song.
When he was felled
shock rocked my earth.
Not Barry.
Not Barry.

He never lost XL essence,
sent a last poem
he thought I'd like.
I did, Barry.
I did.

A zoom wake
with virtual hugs
before he downed
the legal cocktail
laced with poison grace.

Don't tell his wife
suicide is wrong.
Don't tell his friend.
Don't you dare.

21,900 DAYS

The room reeks of lilies and a dirge my mother would hate.
She's dead in that fancy box in front of tear-logged friends
where twelve diaries cluster in secret around her feet.

This is the living litter of words she wrote over six decades.
Gilt-edged pages, five years of one date on each leaf,
packed tight, entry over entry, in her fading pencil script.

I reach under the coffin's half-lid for one leather book,
its suede-soft skin wrinkled as hers. I open it. She speaks.
I open another. She breathes her memories into my heart.

Farm wife woes. Price of a Holiday Rambler. Dreamers Club cake.
Lunch with Phyllis. Arcane runes for menses, expenses.
Daughters she deplored and adored, lifelines entwined with hers.

Should they be buried alive, these words that outlast writers?
Lifting twelve volumes from the satin lining into my arms,
I replace flowers with words in a basket and carry my history home.

WATERMELON GIRL

Broken husband inside at the top of the stairs
awaiting bedpan, fresh bandage, small talk.

Alone in the car at the bottom of the stairs
I'm too hot, too tired till crows scold me to move.

I open the hatch. The watermelon rolls out,
cracks, sweet red meat drains down the drive.

Sitting on a cement step, I weep.
The storm passes. Eyes bleary

I stare at green rind bowls still holding
chunks of deepest red flesh torn from the middle.

I eat it with my hands, sticky juice drizzling down my chin,
consuming the heart like a hunter.

Wiping fingers on my cotton shirt I bend,
lift the grocery bags and climb the stairs.

LAST DANCE

I loved to dance.
He didn't. He wouldn't.
After the amputation
he bemoaned he couldn't.
No second chances in a nursing home.

He cheated at Scrabble
demanded Taco Tuesdays
I shouldn't provide.

Wrote limericks to CNAs,
titillating or what's the point?
Threw ice chips at wraithlike residents
traveling through, touching his belongings.

He stopped mentioning love
when his current situation
became more real than me.

By most measures
I'm better off with him dead.
Better off with him dead.
My mouth fights forming that admission.
What kind of widow says those words?

The pattern I created began
long before his disease.
Planning vacations
selecting workmen
massaging his back
seeing his movies
cheering his teams
putting our dog down alone.

The caregiver role suited us both:
my wiping his tears or whatever,
his expectations as a sultan's due.

It's taken me a decade to lance
this boiling anger at myself.
Near the end of my years,
I'm learning to sway
like a hula kumu
to the haunting
What About Me?

WINTER FARMERS

Solemn men, Great Uncle Jim and Grandpa, bodies still muscled
rise in the drear to milk before dawn. After udders they jumpstart one
Laidlaw from another where buses huddle in the equipment shed.
Farmers drive yellow tin cans when fields yield nothing but snow.

Neither cracks a smile cracking ice from the folding doors.
They hoist themselves to shiver on rigid leatherette seats,
maneuver their coughing buses through wormholes in drifts
eating biscuits from Aunt Lucille and Gramma Donna Belle.

We cousins play war at the roadside, packing snow down backs until
a shuddering bus slides to a stop. We clamber aboard elbowing
other warriors already there hogging seats, blocking aisles.
We tromp on feet, slap heads with pencil boxes, call names:

Willy Chicken Fat, roundest boy, *Sister Sorrowful*, Catholic girl.
Grandpa, his farmer ears better tuned to John Deeres,
delivers this load like bawling calves
who smell more of peanut butter than manure.

We crowd out at the school, shoving each other into the slush.
Grandpa eases the squeaky door closed and off he goes
until he returns at 3 to bring us home again.
He nods at Great Uncle Jim as their routes crisscross.

AUTUMN OF '63
A Pantoum

That November I grow old in my small town.
Too big to fit in with most high school kids
I try out each year. Each year I'm turned down.
I vow not to cry like last year I did.

Too big to fit in with most high school kids,
but *Cheaper by the Dozen* has a role for mother.
I won't have to cry like last year I did.
The role is mine since I'm taller than others.

Cheaper by the Dozen has a role for mother.
I'm naïve. I don't see how playing old lady
(in a role that's mine since I'm taller than others)
is more damning than simply painting scenery.

Too naïve to see playing an old lady
"Disappointed," says the lead, "but I guess you'll do"
is more damning than simply painting scenery.
He kisses me hard in a darkened classroom.

"Still disappointed," says the lead, "but you'll do."
It's meant to hurt. It does. I am scarred.
He kisses me again in that darkened classroom.
Thrown off, confused, untouched, I fall hard.

It's meant to hurt. It does. I am scarred.
The language of love counts the ways.
Thrown off, confused, untouched, I fall hard.
Walking in beauty, I forget who pays.

The language of love counts the ways:
how do I love thee tricks my mood.
Walking in beauty, I forget who pays.
He spreads my secrets from that darkened room.

How do I love thee tricks my mood.
My mother's love sewn in a soft flowing dress
he spreads my secrets from that darkened room
I trade her trust for a boy's caress.

My mother's love sewn in a soft flowing dress
in the autumn of nineteen sixty-three.
I trade her trust for a boy's caress
not knowing that worse is awaiting me.

That autumn of nineteen sixty-three:
dress rehearsal, November twenty-two.
Not knowing that worse is awaiting me.
A President shot on air in full view.

Dress rehearsal, November twenty-two.
A magic bullet, a young widow's crawl,
a President shot on air in full view.
You can't choose how your life lessons will fall.

A magic bullet, a young widow's crawl.
It's a lie that the play must go on.
You can't choose how your life lessons will fall.
A love-sewn dress will never be donned.

It's a lie that the play must go on.
I learn what the refrain of my youth will be.
A love-sewn dress will never be donned.
Lust, grief, and love merge overwhelming me.

I learn what the refrain of my youth will be:
"Where were you when Kennedy was killed?"
Lust, grief, and love merge overwhelming me.
Life's harder to play than a part in Playbill.

“Where were you when Kennedy was killed?”
Innocence died that day on a grassy knoll
Life’s harder to play than a part in Playbill.
The nation’s leading man played his final role.

Innocence died that day on a grassy knoll
I tried out each year; each year I was turned down.
The nation’s leading man played his final role
that November I grew old in my small town.

SADDLE UP

I rummage in the roll top for my precious Big Chief tablet,
round up color pencil stubs in a cottage cheese carton then
belly flop in front of enormous wood cabinet with its tiny TV.

I wait with grade school expectation? exasperation? exaltation?
drawing horses over the lines as wool carpet burns my elbows.
The tube sings a static tune … blooms to black and white

and here they come: stampeding riflemen, tinhorns, card sharks,
Ciscos, Earps, Cheyennes thunder through the living room on
Champion, Diablo, Topper, Silver, Scout and oh, the lyrics,

heroic theme songs! Whistle me up a nobody quicker
on the where do you roam ghostly horsemen riding hell bent
for leather brave courageous and bold when the west was young.

How I want to be one of these lucky buckaroos dashing through
clouds of dust in the gulleys, between lofty canyon walls,
across wide open spaces of my childhood.

Role confusion begins about now. I disdain TV life
of plucky women wrapped in aprons happy while they
churn, sweep, wring, and rake dead gardens back to life.

I want to gallop the range, sing the songs, herd longhorns along,
lift the newborns from the flooded creeks, ride the broncs,
save the day when Sioux come calling with arrows aflame.

My head screams ride like the wind. Mom yells set the table.
I am caught between expectation exasperation exaltation
which has pretty much remained my reality for eight decades.

THE THEFT

The unforgiving virus crept inside
to kill a part of me,
stole a sense at such a harrowing time
and left me scentless,
the weeks
when we all waited to be saved.

Scents locked inside
their elixirs buried deep
tease me now and then,
with faint touch of sweet, tart, spice.

Not a huge loss, not sight or limb
but clothes sun-dried on a line,
dewy earth, mom's L' Air du Temps,
sea gull funk in salt air
pass by unnoticed now.

Memories tell lies and,
as recall amplifies,
I mock my loss.

In this eighth decade
cookies smell sweetest
once they're gone.

PLAYING HENRY FONDA ON A HUMID AFTERNOON

I haven't hunkered at a table
shoulder to shoulder with strangers
since Covid established territorial norm as six feet.
Yet we huddle now in a room so close
we feel each other's body heat,
whiff what we had for lunch.

This could be a séance, I suppose.
A grief group gathered for comfort.
Med students blushing at naked parts
of a body on a gurney.

We are a jury deliberating.
We have struggled with rational emotion
until we are ionized. Exhausted.
Guilty of the need to be done, to run
from mulling a young man's destiny.

As we the jury inch toward mistrial,
the room cools
taut with terribly polite anger.
Stewed coffee smells bitter as the mood.
Jury members lean back,
hands now clasped behind heads.
Open minds solidify to pigheaded.

I never want to walk this graveled path again,
stopping beside the road as the others
march on to some destination
clear as day to them, not even on my route.

RAINMAKERS

It was a perfect union.
Thirteen years we worked together tight as a skin graft.
Detractors said it would never take. Too different they said,
you the ice warrior, me pulsing imagination.

How wrong they were.
We strutted into conference rooms to woo the suspicious
around vast tables of Koa planks or Carrera marble.
We turned those tables on them as their objections dropped
one by one, their little ripe gasps audible to our ears.
Hard for them to take a risk, but they began to hum our tune.

It was seduction.
Skin electric to each other's gesture, glance, lean in now
for the kill. Ears tuned to sounds not even in the room.
Eyes talking to each other as we whispered dreams to them.
We could crack a client like a safe and they ate us up,
you so buttoned down, me so glib
with the gift of making them laugh their way into a snare
of new ideas from a wild rose on a stalk of thorns.

Business sense is real
as any sense of taste smell sound sight touch the brain can feel.
Like traveling preachers we led them to the promised land,
the heights of business class where they longed to belong.
Your starched shirt so white it shouted at a client's eyes
my smile so genuine it eased the sting of signing on dotted lines.

Did our bodies ever blend?
In airport hotel rooms did you invite me in? Did I ache alone
down the hall like a country western rhyme all that time
for the smooth-talkin' man who'd never be mine?
When morning coffee and strawberries were served
and lights dimmed for the meeting to light up in fire,
that's when I was yours and you were mine.
And when we were done we flew home
each to a spouse who asked, "How was the trip?"

SEASONAL AFFECTIVE DISORDER

This is not fertile terrain, these ghost grey clifftops.
Salt wind scrapes meadows high above dark seas

armed with battering ram logs and deadly undertow.
Ground cover struggles to fill damaged patches.

It may not prosper as you have scant room for me,
loving me not how I want but how you can.

BEDTIME

Now I lay me down to sleep.
Alone.
The covers on your side
do not rustle as I am not
a restless sleeper and
require nothing from them,
not even you.
If you should die before I wake,
I will not pray for you.

TATTOO JUNGLE

She is a cutter. Soft skin gives in. Utility knife, scalpel, razor
leaves a thin bloody slice. She's happy about that, at least

she doesn't burn her thighs with cigarette butts or Drano,
burns so much harder to heal, harder to conceal

from a judgmental world. The pain is the same.
It's what she must do to cope, to feel. She hides from

mother's lover's stranger's wondering wandering eyes.
Self-inflicted scars cross nearly everybody's lines.

She disappears in a tattoo jungle. Vines entwine her ankles,
ferns unfurl across her breasts, blossoms nestle between her thighs.

Only I the artist knows within her jungle, wounds thrive so
I choose tips, load my gun. *Another orchid*, we decide.

I am immersed in creation of this walking work of art.
Secret cuts stay secret. With my complicity, she stays alive.

PENINSULA CURRENTS

My husband has gone to sea.
I stood alone the last place we stood together
bid him good-bye scattering ashes riverward.

He's travelled many years in the Strait
in the San Juans in the Charlottes in wind and water currents
whichever way they change and change again.
He is energy and laughter and painlessness
or so I must believe.

The Olympic Peninsula opened its branches to me
as caringly as a nurse log.
I was relieved of my big city past, pace, aggression
allowed to slow with grace.
A hidden sprig of creative now flourishes
with the other mountain wildflowers.

He dances invisibly in the fiber of this nurturing land.
He'll not leave nor will I
a place with greater sense of found than lost.

TRANSCATHETER AORTIC VALVE REPLACEMENT

Our heat pump fails
the day of my sister's heart surgery.
The house grows cold
our renter calls
as I await news in another frigid room
far away from home.

I've sensed my sister's heart all my life,
teasing, sassing, pushing me to grow up.

It beats again today, that heart.
New pump inside old pump
bovine tissue valve open close open close
doing the work of muscle and vein
heart and home both warm once more.

THIS SAFEHOUSE OF MINE

I clamber to the attic
shadow dark as graphic novels,
hearing fearing river dancing rodent feet.

Shuffle stacks of alliteration similes metaphors
rhythms rhymes and what-will-I-use-these-fors.
Grab a wordy handful
some cut deep
slithery as icy market fish thrown for thrills.
Figures of speech yell at me,
Weak words will not protect you now.

Caulk the walls with verse
careful not to toss the spark away
in a bath water of tepid lines.
Words wedged beneath doors
keep disappointment out.
This safehouse of mine,
a Walmart of words,
demands persistence. Endurance.
Will I find what I am looking for today?

Face the picture window.
Inhale hills of bluest salvation.
Bury misery in the fur of a big dog neck.
And write.

Linda B. Myers won her first creative contest in the sixth grade for her *Clean Up Fix Up Paint Up Week* poster. It involved monkeys washing the spots off a giraffe. She doesn't remember what it said and would like to think her words have more staying power these days.

After graduating from Michigan State University and following a career of writing ads in Chicago agencies for national clients, she moved to the Olympic Peninsula of Washington State where she has written ten books—mysteries and historical fiction—all set in the Pacific Northwest. She writes a monthly column for a local newspaper and is a co-founder of Olympic Peninsula Authors. She can often be found being walked by her Great Pyrenees or out-smarted by her Maltese.

Now she has turned to poetry. In *Load-Bearing Walls*, her clear, down-to-earth voice reflects on the people and places that burrow into her memory, not all for the good. We've all been strong supports and had strong supports; this collection will help you recall yours.

www.ingramcontent.com/pod-product-compliance
Lightning Source LLC
LaVergne TN
LVHW090541110826
845146LV00003B/1214